"Sr. Kathleen concludes *Discipline Made Easy* with a listing of beatitudes for religion teachers. I add another: Happy are the religion teachers who read this book, for they are certain to find many valuable tips to improve their teaching."

Dr. Tom Walters
Academic Dean, Saint Meinrad School of Theology

"This book, from a wise and experienced teacher of teachers, is both helpful and necessary. It is full of practical suggestions that will help all teachers, whether beginners or advanced. It is also pervaded by broad understanding, affection, and reverence for the children we are privileged to teach."

Maria Harris
Author, *Teaching and Religious Imagination*

"Kathleen Glavich's book is a treasure for any teacher looking for help to improve discipline in the classroom (and who of us isn't?). Her book presents many examples of typical discipline problems (both small and large) and many techniques (all simple and practical) for dealing with them. But the book is also inspirational, rooting the whole concept of discipline in the reality of our Christian faith and discipleship. Eminently readable, *Discipline Made Easy* does exactly what its title says: It makes discipline easy! I highly recommend it for all teachers."

Melannie Svoboda, SND
Author, *Teaching Is Like...*
Peeling Back Eggshells

"Sr. Kathleen's book is a refreshing approach to maintaining discipline in religion classes. I can hardly wait to use it as an in-service with our teachers. It offers so many useful ideas for new teachers as well as veteran volunteers.

"One of the first fears a new catechist expresses is that of discipline. Sometimes it's the very thing that prevents him or her from volunteering to teach. Sr. Kathleen's book offers excellent practical suggestions for the catechist who wants to discipline with Christian values."

Marianne Slattery
Master Teacher, DRE, Diocese of Cleveland

"Discipline Made Easy is the book I've been looking for since I became a DRE! Discipline is the one issue that hounds most veteran catechists and terrifies most prospective catechists. Time and time again, they have asked me for resources to assist them in the area of discipline. DREs now have a valuable resource to offer.

"Sr. Kathleen approaches discipline within the overall context of the catechetical setting, providing rock-solid techniques without turning catechists into drill sergeants!"

Joe Paprocki
Author, "For DRE's Only" column
in *Religion Teacher's Journal*

DISCIPLINE
made
EASY

POSITIVE TIPS
& TECHNIQUES FOR
RELIGION TEACHERS

Mary Kathleen Glavich, SND

TWENTY-THIRD PUBLICATIONS
Mystic, CT 06355

Second printing, 1995

Twenty-Third Publications
185 Willow Street
P.O. Box 180
Mystic, CT 06355
(203) 536-2611
800-321-0411

ISBN 0-89622-598-4
Library of Congress Catalog Card Number 94-60152
Printed in the U.S.A.

Dedicated to Sister Mary David Horan, S.N.D.,
my teacher,
who disciplined with love

Acknowledgments

Sincere appreciation to

...Sister Mary Agnes O'Malley, S.N.D.,
and Sister Regina Marie Alfonso, S.N.D.,
two outstanding educators who are always willing to
share their knowledge and experience with me
on projects like this book.

...Other Sisters of Notre Dame and friends
who provided me with ideas and help

...The personnel at Twenty-Third Publications
who encourage and support my writing hobby.

Contents

DISCIPLINE
made
EASY

Introduction

*The one who seeks God
must accept discipline.
—Sirach 32:14*

Last year at a catechist meeting for a parish school of religion, the Director of Religious Education introduced Judy, a new catechist. Out of the goodness of her heart, Judy had consented to fill a vacancy in the final hour and teach the sixth grade. Judy stood to acknowledge our applause. Then she pleaded, "I'm petrified. I'm afraid I won't have discipline. Can anyone help me?"

Judy was right to be concerned about discipline. With the change of one word, 1 Corinthians 13:1 becomes a truism for catechists: "If I speak in the tongues of mortals and of angels, but do not have discipline, I am a noisy gong or a clanging cymbal." A's in theology and methods courses, expensive audiovisuals, and hours of preparation are all worthless unless children cooperate. Discipline is essential for teaching. We catechists cajole, coerce, and dazzle children into allowing catechesis to happen. Inability to maintain discipline is the main reason catechists quit. Luckily, discipline is a skill that can be learned, and it can improve with practice. There are strategies that can transform an undisciplined class into a model class.

This book is for new catechists like Judy who are wondering how they will ever manage a class of rambunctious youngsters and teach them something. It is also for catechists who are experiencing major or minor difficulty with discipline. It might even offer seasoned catechists a fresh idea or two to try out this year or give them a new insight into the art of proclaiming the gospel.

In compiling material for this book I asked several teachers and catechists for ideas. One friend replied, "Discipline in religion class? That's easy. All you need is a whip and a chair." I hope you find the suggestions in this book much more helpful for your ministry!

The meaning of discipline

It is no mere coincidence that disciple and discipline share the same root word: the Latin word *discere*, which means "to learn." A disciple is a learner; in the context of a religion class, a disciple is one who is learning about Jesus Christ. Our students are disciples, learners of the Catholic Christian faith and way of life. Would that they were as spellbound by the Good News as Jesus' disciples. When he taught, crowds followed him across lakes and into deserted areas. They even forgot about eating. Some days we're lucky if our students even look attentive.

Discipline is basically a situation that is conducive to learning. It allows all the disciple's energy to be focused on learning. The disciple is motivated to learn, not to misbehave. Discipline sets the stage for success, and success is the best motivator.

Catechists facilitate classroom discipline by managing the physical arrangement and setting the climate for optimum learning to occur. The goal of this external discipline, however, is self-discipline on the part of children. Self-discipline, which requires self-control, enables them to hear the gospel message and absorb it into their lives. It is self-discipline, too, that enables them to live according to the gospel.

By teaching with discipline and ultimately teaching self-discipline, we are preparing students for the Christian life. We are helping them to live like Jesus. As adult Christians with self-discipline they will be better equipped to do these things:

• Get up to celebrate the Eucharist when their bodies crave to stay in a warm and cozy bed
• Listen to others who have different opinions
• Survive trials, pain, and suffering
• Persevere through unexpected setbacks
• Sacrifice for the sake of love—live the way of the cross
• Speak out against injustice
• Bite their tongues when sarcastic comments are on the tip of them
• Be immune to materialism and consumerism
• Reach out to the poor, the suffering, and those who are in distress.

Clearly, establishing good classroom discipline can have far-reaching repercussions in the lives of those we teach. Unfortunately, achieving it today is more of a challenge than ever. Consider the following reasons.

Why children won't behave

Sowing the message of salvation in the hearts of today's children is especially challenging and frequently frustrating because of discipline problems. A fourth-grade catechist reports that her students are so unmanageable that all she can do with them is sing. That in itself is an accomplishment. Another teacher says that her seventh graders think everything is a joke. After religion classes the evening before, day school teachers complain that obscenities are on the board, the electric pencil sharpener is broken, or everything on the teacher's desk has been glued down. No wonder there is a high dropout rate among us.

First of all, society complicates our task by teaching and endorsing values contrary to the Gospel values we teach. By the time children are sitting in our classes, many have already adopted neo-pagan attitudes and practices, not only from the media, but from their friends, neighbors, and families. As the *National Catechetical Directory* points out, "Many Catholics are poorly informed about their faith or have deliberately rejected parts of it" (24). We might just as well be from Mars when we teach that premarital sex is wrong or that self-denial is a good thing. Often, if what we have to say is not denied outright or challenged, it is simply tolerated by those we teach.

Families are on the move

Another factor is the high rate of mobility in the United States, which leaves little chance for a family or child to sink roots in a faith community and be nurtured by it. For most Catholic families the parish is no longer the center of family life. Less than fifty percent of Catholic families go to Mass. In many cases, then, the concepts, the rituals, and the terminology of the religion class are foreign to the children.

Other facts that explain less-than-angelic behavior are related to family life. Too many children are from disturbed or broken families and families that are facing emotional or financial problems. Learning is difficult if not impossible. One out of five Catholic families is now headed by a single parent who probably works. And, in a large percentage of two-parent homes, both parents work. Many children who are left alone for extended periods of time turn to TV for companionship. Television values are questionable, at best, but TV entertains. As a result, children expect to be entertained in religion class.

Another factor is that often "latchkey" children are used to being their own bosses. They resent being told what to do. Naturally, when we take a stand against the wishes of these children, conflict is the result. In the past, when children were reprimanded in school, parents would follow through at home. Today they tend to defend their offspring and ask why the teacher is picking on their child.

Children show less respect

Also, children treat authority figures differently today in general. Though it is a positive thing not to fear adults and those in charge, it is quite another thing to be disrespectful. Parents often unwittingly allow children to confuse lack of fear with lack of respect. In one of my classes, a fourteen-year-old girl named Susie was particularly disrespectful. When I called her mother, I could hear Susie yelling in the background. "Is she fighting with her brothers?" I asked. "No," sighed the mother, "she's talking to me. I don't know what to do with her."

In addition to all these factors, scheduling circumstances make parish religion classes more difficult to control than daily classes. If a religion class is held on a weekday, the children have already spent a whole day in school. They are tired. If classes meet on weekends, the children might have to wake up early. In either case, students have to sacrifice school functions, sports, TV, and other activities. Therefore they may attend class grudgingly and only because their parents make them.

In the light of all these factors, student misbehavior in religion class is understandable. But being understandable doesn't make it acceptable. Our goal should be to establish good discipline: a climate conducive to learning and growth.

Don't get discouraged or give up

Children are in your religion class to learn, and one item of your hidden curriculum is discipline. Children—as we have just seen—do not come programmed to listen, follow directions, share, cooperate, and communicate. Often you have to instill proper behavior by untiringly calling children to it. When the class is restless and talking, instead of just raising your voice to carry over the commotion, stop and deal with the problem. When George yells out for the hundredth time, correct him for the hundredth time.

Once during a school Mass, while one student was drinking from the cup, another student quipped, "Hey, leave some for us!" After the liturgy I captured the boy and roundly scolded him. At one point I asked, "Don't you know how sacred those moments are?" He answered, "I do now."

We struggle to do what is best for the children, and this is not always to their liking. It may not make us popular, but we are not there to be popular. Catechists, like parents, have to sometimes practice tough love. This is painful. Despite personal suffering, we have to stick to principles and teach with a tender tenacity. Jesus wasn't always popular either.

Our task is to use discipline as a tool to form disciples who know the value of discipline. Someday our children may echo the words of actress Julie Andrews: "Some people regard discipline as a chore. For me, it is a kind of order that sets me free to fly."

For Your Reflection

✔How would you rate your classroom discipline?

_____
_____
_____
_____
_____

✔What has discipline helped you to do on a personal level?

_____
_____
_____
_____
_____

✔What particular characteristics of those you teach make discipline a challenge?

_____
_____
_____
_____
_____

Developing Positive Attitudes

The children's story *The Little Engine That Could* conveys a valuable message for life. In case you have forgotten, the little engine conquers a large hill by repeating the words, "I think I can, I think I can...." If we think we can, we can. Our mental outlook to a great extent determines our success or failure. To give an example, if we are walking across a beam and think we will fall, chances are we will. Ever more and more evidence indicates that our physical health is largely a matter of mind. It follows then that positive attitudes toward ourselves and those we teach will yield positive effects. Visualize yourself as a vital and successful catechist, and chances are that is exactly what you will be.

Cultivate a healthy self-concept

The church and in particular the parents of those you teach depend on you to impart the light of faith to young Christians. You have something very precious to hand on—a faith that gives meaning and joy to their lives here and now and that affects their eternal well-being. Furthermore, what you teach them can make a difference in the universal church and in the world.

You can accomplish this significant task if you have good discipline. To have good discipline you need a healthy self-concept. Only then will you be strong enough to exercise leadership in your class.

When your self-esteem is at a low, consider the following: As a catechist you have a special commission. God has chosen and called you to the ministry of teaching religion. As you try your best to fill this role, God will not fail you.

You are a good person. Not everyone is willing to devote time and energy to teach religion for a minimal sum or nothing at all. You have sacrificed television programs, games, and other enjoyable events in order to plan lessons and teach classes. You are giving yourself to your students when you could be with family or friends. You deserve gratitude and respect.

Give yourself reminders

During difficult periods you might not want to go around muttering to yourself "I think I can have good discipline," but you could write one of the following reminders at the top of your lesson plan or put a copy on your mirror or refrigerator where you will see it.

- I am the teacher. They are just kids.
- I am in the strategic position to guide the direction of the class.
- I am older, wiser, more experienced (and maybe larger) than those I teach.
- I have been chosen for this ministry.
- I am loved by God and deserve respect.

In your religion class your whole being should declare that you have a good self-concept: your posture, the way you walk, your voice, your gestures. Everything about you should radiate confidence. Catechists who convey timidity and insecurity invite children to take advantage of them. Children need strong role models. Even in religion class they need a forceful, stouthearted person to take charge.

Sometimes the behavior of children erodes our good self-concept. We begin to think there's something wrong with *us*. Believing we're failures, we become depressed. We dread walking into class. In this situation it helps to talk to someone and even invite an observer to offer an objective perspective and advice.

Determine your teaching style

How you see yourself determines your style of teaching and the atmosphere of your class. Here are some possible self-images. Look them over carefully and decide which, if any, fit you. Check the ones that do. Are they good or bad images?

_____co-seeker of truth   _____witness

_____committed Christian   _____salesperson

_____dedicated teacher   _____police officer

_____general entertainer   _____facilitator

Always be a model

Children need models more than critics. They need people who show what it's like to be made in God's image and likeness, to be redeemed by Christ, and to be a temple of the Holy Spirit. Therefore, they ought to see in you a wholesome pride, hope, courage, and joy. Aim for self-improvement. Know yourself and work to reflect the following Christian virtues:

Patience... to respond calmly to the child who asks in every class, "Why do we have to learn this stuff?"

Understanding... to separate the behavior from the child.

Integrity... to refrain from speaking about children's faults in front of others in the class.

Perseverance... to try again after a lesson fails.

Knowledge... to answer questions or at least to know where to find answers.

Discipline... to teach a good lesson regardless of how you feel.

Love... to cherish your students.

Along with an aura of authority, radiate enthusiasm, joy, and calm. This will help children respect and like you at the same time. When you do not feel enthusiastic, joyful, or calm, rely on the "act-as-if" principle. Acting as if we feel or behave a certain way helps make the feeling or behavior a reality.

Have a high opinion of children

In education courses a favorite story is that of a teacher whose roster contained what she thought were IQ scores. During the year the students she assumed were very intelligent did remarkably better than the rest.

Then she discovered that the IQ scores were actually locker numbers!

Children tend to live up to a teacher's expectations. If you like the children you teach and convey to them that you think they're great, they probably won't disappoint you. Show that you have confidence in them and give them the feeling that you care about them.

Don't let negative attitudes of other catechists color your attitude toward a child or class. Let each year be a new opportunity for the children.

Keep from comparing your present class to classes you had in the past or to other classes. This is especially dangerous if you do it aloud before the children themselves.

Get to know children as individuals

Arrive early so you can chat with children. (They will also realize how important the class is to you if you are early.) Show interest in them. Ask for their opinions and invite their suggestions. In discussions draw from them their experiences, opinions, and feelings. On the first day of class, you might have them fill in a personal questionnaire to inform you of their siblings, their favorite TV show, their hobbies, a unique thing about themselves, and what they think about Jesus, the Bible, the Mass (or whatever you will be teaching that year).

Assume that the children are good. They really want to know about God and their faith. Realize that they are not angels, but neither were you when you were their age. Be aware that discipline problems are usually caused by needs that aren't being met: the need for security or affection, for instance. Many infractions are in reality defense mechanisms. Children who think they are inadequate or unworthy act in unsociable, self-defeating ways. Sometimes they will act impulsively without thinking—just as we sometimes do. Never give up on them. Do your utmost to counsel them and challenge them to be their better selves.

Love your "problem" children

Usually there is at least one child we wish would disappear. This problem child is a challenge to us to be Christlike. Approach the student as a child of God and someone in whom God is living. Reject the behavior not the student. Never show dislike for the student. Pray for an honest love of him or her. Keep in mind the Master Teacher who goes after the lost sheep, and of whom it was said, "A bruised reed he will not break, a smoldering wick he will not quench" (Matthew 12:20). Be prepared to give a second chance, and a third, and a fourth.... The student who is the most difficult has the most need of your love and compassion.

During my first year of teaching religion to ninth graders I felt like a dismal failure. The students constantly challenged what I did and said. They seemed to have little respect for me. In particular, I could count on one bright girl I'll call Barbara, to throw a monkey wrench into my well-planned lessons. Near the end of the year, while correcting tests, I discovered this note Barbara had added to her essay: "Sister, you probably won't believe this, but I go to daily Mass and Communion. Something you said a while ago made me realize how important my faith is."

Not all catechists have a Barbara to reassure them that they do make a difference. Some of us will have to wait for such gratification until the end of time. I imagine many of us will meet our most troublesome students in the heavenly realm and blurt out, "What are you doing here?" It is only then that we'll hear the answer: "Something you said a while ago made me realize how important my faith is."

Difficult students can be like the irritating particle of dust in an oyster which eventually becomes a pearl. Be patient and kind, and the results may surprise you.

If a child has a serious problem, however, get outside help. Professional help may even be needed. If every means has been exhausted to no avail, explore alternative methods of religious education like tutoring, instruction by parents, or moving the child to another class. Your steps may be the best for the child and also prevent him or her from jeopardizing the learning of the rest of the class.

Keep in mind Rabbi Abraham Heschel's observation: "Care is half the cure."

Aim for a comfortable order

Not every catechist recognizes healthy classroom discipline. It is a comfortable order that frees children to learn efficiently. Comfort and order must be in a delicate balance. When either one is overstressed, discipline deteriorates. Two examples of the extremes illustrate this point.

1. Miss Lee sets out to make her hour-long religion class a pleasant experience. She tries to be a pal to her students. She ignores a lot of misbehavior such as talking out because she doesn't want to offend anyone. She lets the students eat in class and have extra free time in order to win their favor. Soon the children aren't listening to her, and learning is blocked. Miss Lee has made things too comfortable. In the end no one is comfortable, least of all, Miss Lee.

2. On the other hand, Mr. Hanson desires to run a tight ship. He seldom smiles or tries anything new for fear the class will get out of hand. Slight infractions are dealt with harshly. Soon children are tense and afraid to exercise initiative or even to ask questions. Learning

again is blocked. Mr. Hanson's emphasis on order has converted children into scared robots instead of Christians who are "an alleluia from head to toe."

Somewhere between these two extremes of anarchy and dictatorship lies a well-disciplined classroom of controlled freedom. Once the catechist recognizes what it is, he or she can pursue it by two means: 1) eliminating any distractions, external or psychological, that hamper the learning process and 2) presenting lessons in such a meaningful and enticing way that students want to do what they ought to do.

Some natural-born teachers achieve a comfortable order automatically. Others of us have to work at it. The quest for good discipline demands self-discipline not only from children but from us as well.

People alive with faith and the joy it brings have the greatest impact on others. You do not have to be a sourpuss or an ogre to have a well-ordered class. Rather, it is the catechist who teaches with zest, love, and a dash of humor who elicits the most cooperation from students. We are delivering the Good News, not the Bad News.

In addition to faith and joy, the following traits won't hurt either:

• *Be professional!* Be businesslike and efficient as you teach. Your style should clearly reflect that class time is important to you.
• *Be confident!* Try to appear confident and sure of yourself even when you are not. Doubtfulness and indecisiveness are detected by children and soon cause problems.
• *Be dressed suitably!* Wearing something better than what you wear around the house shows respect for your students and your role.
• *Be a teacher!* Remember that your role is to teach, not to tell combat stories or deliver monologues on how you

succeeded in business or raised your family.

• *Be dignified!* Don't interpret or react to discipline infractions personally. Maintain your poise even though you may be seething within. Avoid words or actions that are beneath your dignity as a catechist.

• *Be firm and gentle!* Strive to master the art of combining firmness and gentleness, of correcting without crushing, and of stimulating without discouraging.

For Your Reflection

✔How do you feel about your ministry as a catechist?

_____

_____

_____

_____

_____

✔Are you satisfied with the images you checked on page 11? What would you like to see yourself as?

_____

_____

_____

_____

_____

✔What virtues of a catechist do you need to acquire or strengthen?

_____

_____

_____

_____

_____

2

Identifying Potential Problems

Before a stage performance, the director oversees each detail to insure a smooth program. Lines are rehearsed. Costumes and props are tested and put in place. Lighting and sound systems are adjusted. Stand-ins are prepared. While preparing for class, catechists need to be as careful and conscientious as directors in spotting problems and averting tragedies. An ounce of prevention is worth a pound of cure. It is said that ninety percent of discipline problems are preventable. That leaves only ten percent for us to handle.

The *General Catechetical Directory* states "The basic concern of the catechist is to choose and create suitable conditions that are necessary for the Christian message to be sought, accepted, and more profoundly investigated" (71). So, don't ignore serious problems even when dealing with them makes you uncomfortable. You are responsible for insuring that your students can learn.

Check every aspect of the class

✔*Your Teaching Space* A well-prepared environment can prevent discipline problems. Children will find it easier to learn in a clean, neat, organized room, one that is large enough so they aren't crowded but small enough that they aren't lost in it either.

If possible, have the room decorated in the soothing colors of green, blue, and purple, rather than the exciting colors of yellow, orange, and red. Be sure there is good lighting, either above the students' heads or behind them and no bright sun blinding them or creating a glare. There should be sufficient ventilation as well. Always open a window when the room gets stuffy.

Above all, be sure that your teaching space is quiet, conducive to learning and faith sharing. It should be a special sacred space for speaking about God and praying. Children should be able to tell that religion is not just another class. Arrange the room to be attractive, warm, and inviting, and create a congenial, religious atmosphere in the following ways.

• Set up a prayer corner with a Bible, flowers, candles, incense, and a pretty cloth.
• Display inspiring posters.
• Make a religion bulletin board.
• Add a live plant or two.
• Play inspirational music before class and during quiet work times.

• Close the door, pull shades, or close blinds to insulate children from distractions.

Your assigned teaching space may have an unfavorable environment. Do what you can to solve the problems. Here are some typical problems and possible solutions.

If you share a large room with other classes, seat your students so that they can't watch the other classes.

If the room has a distracting or tempting display, make a portable screen from a big packing carton and set it up to block it. Such a "screen" can also be used to hang posters related to the topics being studied.

If you have no blackboard, use a large writing pad and markers.

If you have no overhead projector, make a flannel board by covering a piece of cardboard with flannel. Cut out figures from heavy cardboard and paste a small piece of sandpaper behind them so they will adhere to the flannel.

If the desks or chairs are not suitable, have children sit on carpet pieces or pillows.

✔*Furniture* Seats should be large enough so that the students aren't cramped and low enough so that their feet touch the floor. Tables should have room for knees. Furniture should be arranged so that traffic is no problem. Keep the desks and tables free of student doodling.

A semicircular arrangement of desks is preferable to rows. It is more conducive to discussion and enables you to supervise children more easily and make eye contact with them.

✔*Equipment* Items in this category can be a boon or a bane. When working properly, it is a wonderful teacher assistant. Have all equipment set up, tested, and ready to run before class begins. Avoid tragedies like turning on the VCR for a video on Moses and seeing Paul Bunyan appear on the screen, or having to hunt for a record player that works—after you have the students quieted and prepared to reflect on a sacred song. If setting up equipment wastes class time or if machines are not properly adjusted, children will quickly provide their own entertainment!

Here are some practical tips about equipment.

• Have bulb replacements handy and know how to change them.

• Make sure that everyone can see the screen.

• Keep the board clean and supplied with chalk. If a piece of chalk squeaks, break it in half.

• Use colored chalk for emphasis and interest.

• Return all materials to the proper place so you can find them the next time you need them.

• When depending on equipment that requires batteries or electricity, have an alternate back-up plan in case of power failure.

✔*Class Size* Having too many children in a class may cause problems. Large classes can be divided and taught by different teachers or on different days. If this isn't possible, ask for a teacher's aide or parents to assist you. An extra person can keep an eye on your class when your back is turned, as well as hear prayers and check homework.

Team teaching may be a possibility. Combining two classes frees one person for supervision and management tasks.

The previous year's teacher may be a good resource for advice in dealing with children, especially if your group is large. Remember, though, that children change, and the way they related to another teacher or catechist may not be the way they relate to you.

✔ *Your Schedule* If class meets at a time or on a day that is problematic, try to change it. If a school schedule presents a problem, adapt it. Once I taught in a religion program that scheduled a fifteen-minute recess in the middle of class. The time usually expanded, and the particularly rowdy children usually got into trouble. I cancelled the recess for my class but in exchange let them work on a play, which they loved doing.

Be in your teaching space at least twenty minutes before your class is to start. Begin promptly; don't wait for stragglers. Starting lessons with an interesting activity encourages students to be on time. Look directly at those who attempt to disrupt your lesson, or call them by name and ask them to be quiet.

End class promptly. Linger a while in order to be available to talk with children.

✔*Lesson Content* When children see the value in what they are being taught, discipline is inherently there. Point out why the topics you are teaching are important. Preview material and audiovisuals to spot anything (topics, pictures, scenes) that might cause your class to get restless or disruptive. Plan ahead how to present that potentially disruptive material. For example, a religion class viewed the movie *Brother Sun, Sister Moon* about St. Francis of Assisi. It includes a realistic portrayal of Francis divesting himself of his clothes before the bishop. It would have been good if the teacher had prepared the students for this scene.

✔*Supplies and Materials* Make sure supplies are clean and in working order. Have a few extras on hand in case you need more than you anticipated. This includes worksheets and other handouts.

Provide pencils or pens and collect them after each class. Make them a distinctive color so that you can tell when a student is borrowing one from your desk.

If you are teaching in someone else's classroom, store your supplies in a box that you can carry with you.

✔*Going to Church* If you are planning a lesson in your parish church, or if you will be attending a special liturgy with your class, prepare children ahead of time for what they will be doing. When in church, they tend to sit shoulder to shoulder like sardines, and this can lead to behavior problems. If possible, have them space themselves so everyone is about a yard apart. During a Mass or liturgy, sit behind the students where you can see them.

If your whole program or school is involved, arrange for older and younger students to sit together. Both groups will be better behaved.

✔*Your Teaching Style* A history of noisy or unruly classes indicates that you may be doing something wrong. Know your weaknesses and limitations and decide how to remedy them or compensate for them. For example, you might talk too fast, too slow, or too much. You might have an idiosyncrasy or mannerism that annoys the class. Perhaps you are cross or irritable and you aren't even aware of it.

Sometimes the noise in a class is actually caused by the teacher who slams books closed, walks heavily, slams doors and drawers, teaches in a voice loud enough for everyone in the hall to hear, and uses yelling to discipline. Children tend to imitate this loud behavior, so be sure you don't have such noisy habits.

Aim to be not so much a sage on the stage as a guide at the side. This will keep you from dominating the lesson. Also, you don't have to pretend to know everything. Admit when you have to do some research to answer a question, or better yet, challenge the students to do the research. Be willing to admit it when you make a mistake.

Remove temptations

When you notice students with playthings, rubber bands, notes, and the like, take the things away immediately, but promise to return them to the owners at the end of class.

Use proximity control. When you suspect a child is misbehaving or about to misbehave, move near him or her.

While students are engaged in an independent activity, or while you are conferring privately with one student, situate yourself in the back of the class. Your presence behind the class will deter inappropriate acts because the students will think your attention is still on the whole class.

Make sure you can see the students' hands. If you teach in a room with desktops that open, turn the desks around so that children can't reach into them.

Make note of the children who get into trouble when they are near each other. Separate them and keep them separated.

Always have an activity planned to keep children busy from the first moment they walk in the door, even before the official beginning of class. Give them worksheets, have them prepare scripture readings for class, direct them to sign up on the board for parts in plays.

Have meaningful options ready for those who finish an activity before the rest of the class. Never leave any class unsupervised, no matter what the reason.

Be sensitive to students

Some catechists and teachers fail because they are good at the subject but bad at dealing with children. Thus make a sincere effort to know the characteristics of the age level you are teaching: their developmental stage, their interests, their behaviors.

Get to know children personally and quickly. Learn their names and use them so that each student in your class feels important. Knowing names also gives you a better hold on the class. You might even memorize the roster before you meet the students. This makes it easier to connect names with faces. Find out who needs special attention so they do not disrupt the class. Be alert to students who have special needs because of disabilities. Identify students who have a hard time relating to the others. Get to know the parents and home situations of problem students.

When children enter the room, greet them cheerfully. Pay attention to their conversation and mood. This will alert you to anything that might block their receptivity to your lesson and prepare you to cope with it.

Be sensitive to your students as individuals. Notice that David is down in the dumps and that Melissa has new glasses.

Some discipline problems are related to health. If you suspect that a child has a health-related problem, contact the parents and suggest that he or she have a physical examination.

Notice signs that children are restless or bored during an activity and be flexible enough to change it. When young children are bored, they start fidgeting more than usual and act up. Older students doodle, talk, sigh, yawn, look around, or stare.

Never "project" that you are too busy to be bothered by the children in your religion class.

For Your Reflection

✔ What aspects of your teaching situation are less than perfect? What can you do about them?

_____
_____
_____
_____
_____

✔ How can you make your teaching space more attractive?

_____
_____
_____
_____
_____

✔ Which students in your class do you know least?

_____
_____
_____
_____
_____

3

Starting Off Right

Priscilla was not a good student, and I probably didn't teach her much. But one day during a detention period, she taught me an important lesson. She remarked, "You know, Sister, as soon as a teacher walks into the room we can tell if she can handle us." Discipline is largely a matter of beginnings: our opening class, our lessons in the blueprint stage, our readiness for the students, and our preparation of the environment and equipment.

Good classroom management and discipline begin with day one. That first class is as crucial as the opening show of a TV program. Often it determines whether or not we will hold an audience.

You never get a second chance to make a good first impression, and what impression do we want to make? We want to appear businesslike but caring, efficient but relaxed, knowledgeable but open to the students' ideas. Above all we want to be someone children can trust. Begin to build a good student-teacher rapport by your friendliness.

Always teach something in the first class. On the first day you will have your students' attention more than in succeeding days. Take advantage of it. Also, by moving directly into the subject, you let children know you mean business.

Deal firmly and quickly with any incidents that arise on the first days or you will lose credibility. It is almost impossible to restore order if you begin with a casual, lenient attitude.

Know where you are going

In Lewis Carroll's *Alice in Wonderland* Alice converses with the Cheshire Cat.

Alice asked, "Would you tell me, please, which way I ought to go from here?"

"That depends a good deal on where you want to get to," said the Cat.

"I don't much care where—" said Alice.

"Then it doesn't matter which way you go."

Unlike Alice, we catechists must have our destination clearly in mind. As we lead our students on the year's journey, our goals are our guide. Before class begins, use your manual to decide what you want your students to know or do by the end of the year. Think big.

For example, a fifth-grade teacher might set this goal: I want my students to grow in appreciation of the sacraments, especially the Eucharist. Formulate your goals in a few statements.

Having a sense of direction will make you more conscientious and determined.

Set the tone and expectations

Before the school year begins, send your students post-cards welcoming them to your class. If you don't have your class list early enough to do this, prepare a hand-written note for each child, making each slightly different. Distribute the notes the first day. This will set a nice tone to the class and begin a good relationship between you and the children.

Share your hopes and goals for the year. Stress the importance of the class. Convey high expectations for your students. To expect mediocrity is an insult. Tell them you expect them to bring their books to class, you expect them to come on time, and you expect them to participate in class. Insist that they do neat work. Keep your standards high. Expressing hope and expectation works like a self-fulfilling prophecy. "I know you'll show the younger children how to act during Mass" gets better results than "Those of you who act up during Mass will be in big trouble."

A traditional adage is "Don't smile before Christmas." Although we definitely should not take that advice literally, there is wisdom behind it. A teacher must be businesslike and not over-friendly until class control is secured. The first few weeks are comparable to a honeymoon. Then classes sometimes test the teacher. By Christmas the teacher should have firmly established discipline.

Try to create a classroom family. With the right guidance you and those you teach will form bonds that will be expressed in mutual concern and support.

Set realistic rules

Sometimes children will honestly not know what your idea of good classroom behavior is unless you spell it out. In one of my classes several children persisted in calling out answers. I discovered that at the school they came from the teacher encouraged this.

✔*Declare the rules that will hold in your class* and review the school or program rules. The students need to know their limits. If you don't define them, they will seek them by trial and error.

✔*Give the reasons for the rules.* There is quiet in the hall out of courtesy for other classes. In class there is no gum chewing because you don't like it and your wishes are to be respected, and more practically because gum tends to end up on desk bottoms, on the floor, and under shoes.

✔*Let children know you are concerned* that they are safe and secure in the classroom. Explain that rules create a good climate for learning. Children actually appreciate reasonable rules; they know that they are for their own protection and benefit. They also appreciate having the rules enforced. Students aren't really happy if they can run all over the teacher and get away it. Moreover, when one or a few students break the rules without censure, the rest of the class is frustrated and angry—and rightly so.

✔*Inform children of the consequences* of not keeping the rules or at least have these clear in your own mind. Penalties issued on the spur of the moment in the heat of anger could easily be disproportionate to the offense.

✔*Allow democratic participation.* Let children share in the formulation of the rules as well as in determining the consequences of breaking them. This will give them ownership of the class. It will also somewhat relieve you of the job of being the enforcer since punishment will be the natural result of a transgression. In determining punishment for a specific incident, however, take into consideration the unique needs of individuals and the circumstances of the situation.

✔*You might have children sign a contract* accepting responsibility to abide by the rules. Send home a letter explaining school and classroom policies so that parents are informed about your class and can support you.

✔*Post the class rules where everyone can see them.*

Here are some rules about rules: State them positively. For example, instead of saying, "Do not chew gum," say, "Throw any gum in the wastebasket before class." Rather than, "Do not mark up your books," say, "Show respect for your religion books. Keep them clean."

State the rules briefly so that they are more easily remembered. For instance, "Be kind." Make no more than five rules. The fewer the better. A multiplicity of rules multiplies problems. A teacher I know has just one good rule: "Only one person speaks at a time." This means that when the catechist or a student speaks, everyone else listens.

All rules should facilitate learning. If there is no good reason for a rule, don't make it.

Have a seating plan

Start out the year by having a seating plan with the students in alphabetical order to help you remember their names. Later when you know them, arrange their seats strategically. Seat a child who is habitually tardy near the door. Separate children who are like fire and dynamite when they are together. Put troublemakers in the front near you.

After you know your class, you may decide to let the children choose their own seats. Always be ready to change a seat if necessary. Keep an up-to-date seating plan handy for substitute teachers.

Establish routines

Introduce routines and put them into practice immediately to prevent wasted time and needless frustration later. In advance, decide the most efficient way to accomplish routine tasks. Assure children that classroom policies are not absolute rules. Exceptions may be made when necessary. Routines that save time and create order in a classroom include the following.

• *Beginning class* Many catechists like to begin with prayer. You might prefer to pray within a lesson and begin class instead with a joke, a simple call to order, or twenty seconds of silence.

• *Assigning hooks or lockers* Coats and jackets should be out of the way. Tell children to put their books under the desk until they are needed. Their desks should be cleared of everything at the beginning of class so that they are free to concentrate on the class.

• *Taking attendance* Call names and have children respond, "Here" or take attendance informally, scanning the class before the lesson begins.

You might teach children to take attendance. Have their names on slips of paper cut into different shapes. Place these by the door. As they enter the room, they find their name and place the paper through a slot into a box. Be creative in designing shapes for the attendance slips and the locations in which to put them. For instance, children can pick up a flower slip and put it into a garden or vase. You might designate an area on a bulletin board "In" and "Out." Tack individual slips under *Out*. When the students arrive, they move their names to the *In* spot.

• *Raising hands to answer* The practice of raising hands allows one child to answer at a time so that the answer is heard and understood. Avoid repeating a student's answer. This discourages children from listening to one another. Furthermore, they should speak loud enough for everyone to hear.

• *Distributing and collecting papers and supplies* The way you distribute and collect materials will depend on the size of your class and your seating arrangement. The important thing is to make your chosen procedure a habit. Papers and supplies can be distributed by the first person in each row and collected by the last person.

To save time you might have children pick up books, papers, and supplies as they enter the room. Similarly, instead of collecting these materials, have children deposit them in an assigned place as they leave class.

• *Passing in papers* If your class is in rows, have the papers passed up from the back to the front. Then have the student in the first seat of the first row collect them across the front and put them on your desk. You may wish to have children bring up their papers individually as they are finished to give them a little exercise after a quiet activity. To prevent squabbles, remind children always to put their names on papers and art projects.

• *Sharpening pencils* It's best to have children sharpen their pencils before class. Keep extra pencils on hand to replace those that break during the lesson. Direct children to leave a personal belonging in place of the borrowed pencil on the desk as a reminder to return it.

• *Distributing and collecting books* Appoint a child in each row or group to distribute and collect books or have them on the children's desks ahead of time. If children have their own books or Bibles, make sure their names are on them the first day, thus avoiding mix-ups.

• *Going to the rest room* Children should take care of going to the rest rooms before class. Allow for emergencies, however. You'll find that when students ask to go to the rest room during class or out to get a drink of water and you ask, "Can you wait?" they usually respond, "Yes" and return to their seats.

• *Moving from place to place as a group* Establish stopping places for the leader so that any stray students can merge again with the group. Bring up the end of the line yourself.

• *Establishing groups* Assign children to groups. Be prepared to change the groups during the year. Let different children experience being a group leader.

• *Straightening up the room after class* Make children responsible for cleaning up their own territory. Appoint helpers to wash the boards.

• *Assigning jobs* Choose children for various jobs. The more you can involve the better. They can close the door at the beginning of class, take the attendance slip to the office, answer the door, distribute papers, pass the wastebasket, and operate equipment.

Give jobs to hyperactive students, shy students, or students who crave attention. Use these jobs as privileges which can be given or taken away as a means of disciplining.

Develop positive relationships

Don't just teach a class, teach children. Get to know them on a one-to-one basis and develop a good relationship. You might be the only friend some children have. They will not be likely to do anything to spoil that relationship.

Express sympathy to your students in time of illness

or misfortune. Call, send a card, or visit them. Also, let children get to know you. Be willing to share yourself with the class. If you play the guitar, use it in a lesson. If you are artistic (and even if you're not), make souvenir cards for your students for Christmas or as prizes or surprise gifts.

For Your Reflection

✔ What rules in your classroom are the students aware of? What input have they given to these rules?

_____
_____
_____
_____
_____

✔ What routines need to be set in your class? Where will you start first?

_____
_____
_____
_____
_____

✔ Are you usually consistent with your routines? If not, why not? How do children react to them?

_____
_____
_____
_____
_____

4

Creating Your Own Techniques

A fifth-grade teacher where I once taught was having difficulty with an exuberant redhead named Jim. In desperation, she taped a green scapular under his desk, hoping that Mary would help her. The scapular remained until one day when the teacher had objects hidden around the room and told the class to find them. Jim assumed that the scapular he discovered under his desk was one of these objects and claimed it as a prize. Whether or not the scapular affected Jim's behavior in class is unknown. The last I heard of him he was running for a government office.

Unless you diligently employ tactics for good discipline from September to June, even a class that begins like a dream can deteriorate into a nightmare. You do not have to be domineering and overbearing to have good discipline—a master instead of a minister. A master forces students to behave; a minister guides and encourages them. Each teacher and catechist has to develop techniques that are right for him or her. These come naturally or are learned from other teachers. Of course the ideal strategy is to make yourself so well-liked that children wouldn't think of displeasing you!

The following are some ways to survive now that classes are no longer "taught to the tune of a hickory stick." Always begin with the gentlest form of discipline and if that fails, resort to a stronger method. Your most drastic measure soon becomes the standard.

Use nonverbal signals

Most of us have a repertoire of nonverbal signals. These enable us to get a point across without disturbing the class. There is the classic stern look, which you can practice in a mirror. Other teacher looks include warning, questioning, dismay, disapproval, anger, amazement, and shock. A raised eyebrow, a hard stare, a certain smile, a waving finger, or a mere shake of the head are also no-fuss ways to quell misbehavior.

Send messages by means of gestures. Glance at an offender and point to the chart of rules. Develop codes. Pointing to the wastebasket means "Throw out the gum." Pointing to the floor and making an upward sweep with the hand means "Pick up the paper." Putting your finger over your lips means "Quiet." A thumbs-up means "That's good." Drawing your finger across your neck means "Watch it!"

If a student is not working at an assigned task, quietly go to him or her and touch the textbook or worksheet. Often this is all that is needed. A friendly hand on the shoulder or a nonthreatening touch on the arm will also prompt students to get down to business.

Write a misbehaving child's name or initials on the board. This will usually stop the disruptive behavior and it will remind you to speak to the child later.

Children will appreciate your tact in disciplining. Someone defined tact as "raising your eyebrow instead of the roof."

To restore calm in the midst of chaos one teacher stood on her desk and got everyone's attention. A dramatic move like this should be used sparingly. It soon loses its shock value.

To alert misbehaving children that you know what is going on, change your voice as you are teaching. Slow down, increase the volume, lower the tone, speak very deliberately, or insert a meaningful pause. Do not, however, shout or raise the pitch of your voice. Little children respond well to a whisper.

Reprimand privately

Often it is better to reprimand privately. This does not distract children who are working. It also prevents the guilty party from being a martyr in the eyes of the class.

Suppose you see a child making an airplane out of your carefully prepared worksheet. Go to the culprit's desk and whisper something like:

"Are you learning?"

"Is what you're doing helping the others to learn?"

"What are you doing?"

"What should you be doing?"

"Can you do it?"

"Will you do it now?"

Keep children on task by making statements that are motivational rechargers. For example, if you see a child daydreaming, instead of working an exercise in the textbook, whisper, "The sooner you finish, the more time you'll have for yourself."

Sometimes you can catch a student's eye when he or she is about to throw a spitball and just say, "Un-uh," or an emphatic "No!" without interrupting the lesson.

If you speak to a child privately in front of the room, position yourself so the offender's back is to the class, and you can still see the other children.

Cultivate a sense of humor

Children like teachers who can tell or take a joke. Spice your lessons with a bit of humor now and then. Laugh with children when something humorous happens. Be able to laugh at yourself. It makes you more human and approachable.

Most of us resist being told what to do. Orders can make us angry or feel degraded. Students will respond to reminders positively if they are delivered with a note of humor. To hurry her class along when they are moving to church, a teacher friend of mine says, "My grandmother walks faster than you." When it looks as if someone is looking at someone else's paper, she says, "This is not the time to do eye exercises." The students get the point.

Sometimes you might be able to kid students out of ill-humor or away from misbehavior.

When a guest speaker was to address my twelfth graders, I was concerned about the class clown. Bob was well over six feet tall and large. (One day during homeroom period he fit a whole apple in his mouth!) By contrast, I am a size 8 petite. Right before the speaker was to arrive, I walked over to Bob and whispered, "If you make one comment out of line, I will break every bone in your body." This ridiculous, unorthodox remark shocked him into silence.

Plan a signal for getting attention

When you want the class's attention, simply say, "If I could have your attention please," or use a signal like clapping your hands, ringing a special bell, playing a chord or a little tune on the piano, flicking the lights off and on, or whispering. A teacher I know puts her hands behind her head. One by one the children imitate her until everyone is ready.

Warn children before it is time to conclude an activity so they have the satisfaction of completing it. Announce, "You have three more minutes" or "Start putting on the finishing touches."

Give and take "time out"

Little children who need time out because of misbehavior can be invited to cool down at a special table, in a special chair, or on a throw rug. Older children, too, can benefit from being set apart from the group for a while to think things through.

At times your entire class can become unruly. When this happens, stop teaching. Firmly state, "I'm waiting." If this has no effect, walk over to your desk and be seated. Pretend to be engrossed in correcting papers, looking over the manual, or some other task. Eventually the children will realize that you refuse to teach over their noise. Gradually they will settle down and look at you. Once there is silence, look up and ask, "How many are ready to learn something?" Undoubtedly every child's hand will be raised.

Use awards

"Bribery" works on all grade levels. For instance, agree to do something the children enjoy if there is one-hundred percent cooperation during a difficult lesson. Peer pressure will come into play here—for the good.

Entice the students with creative promises. To persuade eight-year-old Kevin to eat his baloney sandwich, I told him I would Indian wrestle with him. After lunch we went behind a screen in the office and had our match. I lost—but only because the principal was peering over the screen and making me laugh. For the rest of the year this shared "secret" made Kevin and me friends.

Remember that extrinsic motivation is not as powerful or as lasting as intrinsic motivation. Try to spur your children on to be good students for the sake of the sheer satisfaction, enjoyment, or challenge of it. Rewards and punishments may work momentarily but then have no significant influence on the children's lives. Our goal is not merely to control behavior during the time the children are in our class, but to form attitudes and convictions.

Talk with the class

Communication is one of the most effective means to prevent as well as solve problems in offices, in homes, and in classrooms. Now and then take time to talk with your class apart from the lesson discussions. When you openly discuss what is underlying classroom happenings, you will be building rapport and creating a feeling of community.

If the children are affected by something that has just occurred, talk about it for a while—a short while. For example, if they have just witnessed a car accident or the first snowfall of the season, don't ignore these experiences, but comment on them. The minds of the children will be centered on them anyway. Sometimes unexpected events are opportunities to teach lessons that will last a lifetime.

Give the class a pep talk on behavior when you sense they need one. Motivate them to learn. Review the reasons for rules. Urge them to be mature and smart. Assure them of your care and support.

After some misfortune has occurred as a result of misbehavior, discuss the incident with the students to make it a learning experience.

Call misbehavers by name

When reprimanding someone before the class, use the student's name. Be brief in your rebuke. A public scolding has a ripple effect. Other children will avoid the misbehavior.

Sometimes it is sufficient merely to state what the student is doing wrong in order to change behavior: "Carol, you're talking."

In calling attention to a misdeed, make the problem the child's, not yours. Ask, "What did you do? What are you going to do about it?" Do not ask, "Why did you do this?" The child probably doesn't know.

Avoid reprimanding an individual repeatedly or at length during class. A curt "That's enough!" may be sufficient.

To recapture the attention of children who are talking or daydreaming, call on them. (Note that children who have attention disorder deficit [ADD] can be looking out the window but hear everything you say. Ask a question and they will prove it.)

Change a child's seat during a lesson if necessary.

Divert a child who is misbehaving with a question. If Andy is poking the student in front of him. Ask, "Andy, what part of the assignment did you find hardest?" or "Andy, would you please erase the board for us?"

Use students' misbehavior to your advantage in a clever way to reinforce what you are teaching, surprise the class, and add new vitality to the lesson. For instance, suppose as you are talking about sharing our goods with others, Tommy is playing with a calculator he brought to class. You walk up to him saying, "Christians are willing to share, just like I know Tommy is willing to give me this calculator for a little while. Tommy, I need your calculator. May I please borrow it?" Accept the calculator from Tommy and take it to your desk.

Be creative in giving positive orders

Commands express power, and power may evoke hostility or fear in children. Therefore, when you issue orders, disguise them; for example, instead of saying, "Turn to page 64" say, "The story is on page 64." Instead of saying, "Write a paragraph" say, "You will write a paragraph."

Likewise state warnings and reprimands positively. For example, instead of saying, "You're getting too noisy. Quiet down," say, "This writing activity needs concentration. Let's not talk during it."

Use the cooperative approach in giving an order. "*We'll* need to do this." "*We* need to move quickly and quietly."

When children are not doing something they should be, ask them to do it rather than ordering them: "Would you please pick up that paper?" not "Pick up that paper."

Beware of giving directions that assume the children are working for you not themselves. Avoid beginning orders with, "I want you to," "I need," or "I'd like you to."

Soften an order by pointing out when or where the children can do what they want: "Julie and Dawn, you can finish your conversation in ten minutes when class is over." "Bob, you can use that language at home, but not in this room."

Give incorrigible children papers on which to record each time you must correct them. This will help them realize how often they disrupt the class. It will also serve as a means of tracking progress.

Have private talks with misbehavers

The most effective way to deal with misbehaving children is to talk with them privately. This personal approach is less embarrassing for the student. It is more honest because the child will not be performing in front of his or her peers. It saves precious class time. Furthermore, devoting extra time to a child sends the signal that you really care. At the end of a private talk children should feel good about themselves and you.

Plan your talks to be positive and to reflect care for the child. Disarm with your opening statement instead of beginning with an attack. Say something like "I'm concerned that something is bothering you" or "This isn't like you. What's wrong?"

First, make the guilty party aware of the problem unless he or she obviously knows what is wrong. Be firm and make it clear that you will not allow certain behavior in class. You have a responsibility to the whole class that learning is able to take place.

Second, lead the offender to reflect on how his or her behavior is affecting others and suggest how to make up for any wrongdoing. Guide the child to realize that the wrongdoing has actually hurt him or herself.

Third, get the child to accept responsibility for his or her behavior and cooperatively determine how to eliminate the undesirable behavior, spelling out actions and consequences. Motivate the child to take steps to change by asking, "Do we have to make a big deal out of this, or can we handle it ourselves?" Before the next class it helps to remind the student of the plan.

Forced apologies are rarely effective because they are probably insincere. If a child has hurt another child or

the whole class, suggest an apology but don't encourage
hypocrisy.

Guidelines for a conference
Throughout a student conference try the following.

• Ask questions and listen to the child; really listen.
These five questions, for example, would be very ap-
propriate:
   What if everyone in the class did what you did?
   What would your classmates say about what you did?
   How are things going with you?
   How is your behavior affecting others?
   What can I do to help you?
• Handle the child with gentleness and acceptance.
• Look into the child's eyes as you speak. Smile once
in a while to signal acceptance.
• Make supportive statements like "I don't want the
class to think badly of you" or "Let's see what we can do
to lick this problem."
• Appeal to the child's desire to be mature and well
liked.
• Plant seeds for further thought with brief comments
like "If I were you, I wouldn't want to hurt my future"
or "Do you really think this is true?"
• Strive to preserve a good relationship so that learning is not blocked for the future.

Move around the room
While children are working independently or in small
groups, circulate not only to supervise but to answer
questions and to be of assistance. Some mischief is the
result of students' not being able to accomplish a task.
Their frustration is expressed in the form of inappropriate behavior.

When a child is not working, ask, "Are you having trouble?" or "Is this too hard for you?"

A pat on the head, a hand on the shoulder, or a hug goes a long way in reassuring children that you care about them and that they count. One teacher stands at the door and shakes each student's hand as a sign of peace when the class leaves.

Physical restraint might occasionally be necessary to keep children from harm. Be careful and speak soothingly to a child by saying things like, "Take it easy. Everything will be all right. Just calm down."

Corporal punishment is not an option today. Don't use it.

Have children write

Have perpetrators write reports about what happened. These reports provide a cooling-off period for the students and you. They can also be used in conferring with parents. During a conference with the child discuss what was written.

As a form of punishment, have the children write essays about the pros and cons of their misbehavior. This will cause them to think about what they did and may change their behavior.

Periodically solicit feedback from children by passing out stationery and asking them to write you a letter about the class. They could tell you their feelings, make observations, ask questions, or write anything they would like to share with you. Assure them that what they write will be confidential unless you need someone's help to answer a situation in the letter.

Put a suggestion box in your room so that children can have input. Sometimes their ideas and even their complaints can make us better catechists and teachers. You may find notes saying, "Go fly a kite" or worse, but offering children a chance to express their thoughts is worth the risk.

Pray often with children

Sincerely pray with your students, not just formal prayers, but spontaneous prayer and centering prayer. Some teachers gather children in a prayer circle with arms around one another and pray for intentions. Praying expresses and helps to create Christian community. The stronger your ties are with the children as a group, the better chance you have of being a formative influence on their behavior.

Do not feel guilty about giving children silent time in class for personal prayer. This might be the only time they pray.

Don't make God an enforcer

When reprimanding children do not speak of God in such a way that they come to think of God as the all-seeing eye ready to zap them for any transgressions. God's reputation is easily ruined by statements such as, "God's watching you" or "What would God say?"

Lecturing, preaching, and moralizing during a time of correction work more harm than good. They evoke animosity, which leads to even more disorderly conduct.

Instead, communicate in a firm, matter-of-fact way. If you speak with a hesitant, timid, or pleading voice, you lose ground. If you are indecisive, vacillating, or look helpless, your authority weakens.

Don't tolerate private conversations or slovenly work. Challenge children to meet your expectations.

For Your Reflection

✔What are some techniques you remember from your experiences as a student? Do you use these now?

_____

_____

_____

_____

_____

✔What new techniques discussed in this chapter would you like to try in your class? What will you do first?

_____

_____

_____

_____

_____

✔In what ways do you talk about God with those you teach? Do you ever put God in the role of enforcer?

_____

_____

_____

_____

_____

Instilling Mutual Respect

5

Imagine this scenario. A fifth-grade teacher is talking about the greatest commandment. "Jesus told us to love one another.... Jerry, if you don't stop picking on Vicky, I'm going to start picking on you.... This is the second greatest commandment, that we love one another.... Bob, who do you think you are that you can keep interrupting this class? And you, young lady, you wipe that smirk off your face. ...Jesus said that the sign that we are Christians is that we love one another."

A class like this would make any lesson completely forgettable. A teacher should be a helpful, caring, competent, reliable, admirable person, someone children look up to and imitate. When we fail to act with respect, when we are rude, unreasonable, and unfair, we lose the students' respect. Even worse, they will mirror our behavior.

The way teachers treat us and speak to us stays with us for life. I can vividly recall my fifth-grade teacher's stinging comment when I wasn't able to answer a question in history class: "Glavich, you don't know beans from butter with the bag wide open." I never liked history much after that.

Realize that often it is not *what* you say but *how* you say it that makes the difference between respect and disrespect.

If our discipline methods are merely displays of power that intimidate children and render them powerless, how can we teach Jesus' message of having a heart for the poor and living the Beatitudes?

Following are some practical ways to model good behavior, teach in a truly Christian setting, and enjoy good discipline all year through.

Some don'ts for teachers

Shun verbal abuse, which undermines your authority rather than reinforces it. Above all, it alienates children. Don't nag, lose your temper, use sarcasm, humiliate or embarrass children, threaten, ridicule, insult children, call them names, or try to have the last word. You may be able to crush a troublemaker with one brilliant, withering remark; but consider what children learn when you resort to such methods to control them or to defend yourself.

Avoid yelling. It is upsetting and casts a pall over the whole class. If you shout at the slightest provocation, either you are ignored or you unwittingly set up a game in which children delight in goading you to the exploding point. On the other hand, if you usually speak calmly, when you do raise your voice a notch, children will be startled and listen.

Resist being drawn into futile disputes or arguments with a child. You may well be the loser in the class's opinion.

Never touch misbehaving children or grab an article from them. Such actions might unintentionally hurt them.

Avoid confrontation. The child might win. Try not to be placed on the defensive.

Don't "dare" children. They are likely to take you up on it, and then you have to follow through.

Avoid using grades as a threat. This is never a good way to motivate children—especially in religion class.

Don't punish the whole class for the infraction of one child or a few. It is unjust to punish the innocent.

Avoid forced confessions. The accused student will probably lie. Simply state that you know what the child has done and you don't want it to happen again.

Don't use empty threats like "If you don't finish that paper, you'll stay here all night." This kind of threat is dishonest and ineffective. Children know you don't mean it, and some of them see a threat as a challenge! If you do threaten a student, carry it out.

Don't overreact to minor infractions by delivering a grand tirade. When you see a child chewing gum after supposedly throwing it away, or when another student counters your directions with "Why should I? It's a free country, isn't it?" it might take the control of a saint not to shake the little monster until his or her teeth rattle. You are more apt to make an issue of a trivial matter if you are tired or in poor health.

Don't assign homework as a punishment. It may cause children to dislike the study of religion.

Don't interrupt a child who is speaking or answering a question.

Never belittle a child's answer. Not only will the child be embarrassed if you do this, but other children may be discouraged from answering. Try to find something good to say about every sincere response.

Avoid making a scene in class for the sake of your ego and your own needs, for example to protect your power.

Don't take out personal problems on children. Leave your troubles outside the classroom. Be especially patient when you are having a down day. If you do lose control of yourself, an apology affords children the respect they deserve and teaches a powerful lesson.

Refrain from speaking about the faults of your students and their families unless you are honestly trying to help them. This is a matter of professional ethics.

Some do's for teachers

Always be polite with children. Use please, thank you, and you're welcome frequently when talking to them. Common courtesy should be a ground rule in your classroom.

Respond to infractions quickly and fairly. Children understand and accept this kind of action.

Be consistent. Children need the security of knowing what to expect. If talking out in class warrants a reprimand one week, it deserves one the next. If a humorous remark makes you laugh at the beginning of class, it shouldn't be cause for detention at the end of class. If Tina is late and is punished, Tony should be punished for coming late, too. Mete out punishments objectively. To children unfairness in a teacher is a mortal sin.

Make disciplinary actions constructive. Writing "I will not talk" a hundred times on the board doesn't accomplish much except dirtying the board. Match the punishment to the crime if possible. For example, a student who writes on the desk should have to clean it and maybe the other desks in the room as well.

Focus on solutions. Suggest ways to make things right.

Discuss the action, not the personality. Correct, criticize, or condemn the unacceptable behavior, not the child. This preserves their self-esteem. Say, "You have never finished an exercise on time," not "You are lazy."

Give opportunities to save face. Offer alternatives. Children need to feel important and significant, too. Sometimes you might have to back off. When a child says something disrespectful, delay reacting. Then ask "I don't think I heard you correctly. What did you say?" Chances are that the child will retract the statement or apologize.

In confronting students, use "I-statements" rather than "you-statements." Beginning with *you* is accusing. Instead of "You are disrupting the whole class by your comments," invite a response by expressing your feelings and saying "I find it hard to teach when I'm constantly interrupted," or, "I am angry because of what is going on." When children know that a teacher is troubled by their behavior, they usually want to correct it.

End serious misbehavior promptly by saying "Stop it," "That's enough," or "We don't do that." Recommend that the children quit before they get into more trouble. Then minimize rather than maximize the situation.

Stop individuals from jeopardizing the learning of the others. Simply say, "Please see me after class" and move on. To put an end to a verbal battle, say, "We'll continue this conversation after class."

Keep your dignity and defuse dangerous situations by using humor.

Convey affection for children even when reprimanding them. You might even say, "I like you, but I don't like this behavior."

Let bygones be bygones. Forgiveness is the child's

means to regain self-esteem after making a mistake.

Remember that your goal is not to punish children but to facilitate discipline. You do not want to change just surface behavior, but basic attitudes.

For Your Reflection

✔In what ways might you show more respect for those you teach?

_____

_____

_____

_____

_____

✔Is your method of dealing with discipline problems mature? Is it Christian? Can you think of actual examples of successful discipline techniques you have used? What are they?

_____

_____

_____

_____

_____

✔Which of the do's and don'ts listed in this chapter especially apply to you? What will you do about them from now on?

_____

_____

_____

_____

_____

Presenting Fascinating Lessons

6

Most catechists and teachers agree that the strongest form of preventive discipline is good lessons. A good lesson takes time to prepare. Very few people can successfully talk off the top of their heads while standing in front of a class. Children are quick to detect that the teacher is unprepared and proceed to carry out their own plans.

A well-planned lesson is usually interesting, taught with enthusiasm, and helps one to teach with confidence. Consequently it holds children's attention, and they have neither the time nor the desire for disruptive behavior.

A teacher who cares plans care-fully!

Prepare well

Advance preparation is essential. All the good will in the world won't substitute for it. Imagine a surgeon going into an operating room without preparation, or a football team going onto the field without a strategy. We who are dealing with the faith and spiritual well-being of other human beings have an obligation to prepare. Try to spend at least twice as much time preparing a lesson than you spend teaching it.

Those who try to teach relying solely on the spontaneous inspiration of the the Spirit, soon find their students following the lead of other spirits. Normally the Spirit works through us when *we* work. Preparation takes time and effort, discipline, and even sacrifice. But the rewards are worth it.

When we have a sound plan and are familiar with it, our teaching flows smoothly with no awkward pauses and fumbling for pages. Students do not have time to get into mischief. If we are unprepared, while we are hemming and hawing and paging through the manual, not only is the clock ticking away, but Joey is gluing together the pages of someone else's religion book.

In addition, when we are prepared and have made the lesson our own, we are more confident and automatically convey this to the children. They sit up and take notice.

Ways to insure good lessons

✔*Make them long enough.* Don't be caught with minutes to spare at the end of your lessons. Always plan more than you will need. Have an additional activity on hand to fill the time, perhaps a review game or project.

✔*Keep lessons unpredictable.* Keep children guessing. They should never know what to expect when they walk in the door for your class: games, independent work, art projects, discussion, group work, a video, a guest speaker. Remember that everyone likes novelty. More important, presenting materials in various ways meets the needs of children who have different learning styles. How many ways can you think of to have children read a page in their books? (Students read the page silently; you read it for them; they read it aloud together; they listen to a tape; one child reads the page aloud; each child reads a paragraph—or a sentence!—going around the class in order; children read when called at random.) Allow poor readers a chance to "pass" to spare them embarrassment.

✔*Keep them varied.* Change activities in the course of a lesson. The younger the children, the more often change is needed. In general, children's attention spans match their age. According to this rule of thumb, a five-year-old has a five-minute attention span and a thirteen-year-old has a thirteen-minute attention span. For a change of pace, play a review game, learn a song, say a prayer, or hold class in a different location. The possibilities are endless; you just have to think of them.

✔*Make them interesting.* The material should be interesting. A good lesson engages children's minds and hearts by relating to them, and it impels them to think and to respond. They usually find anything relevant to their lives interesting. Make the effort to link what is being studied with their culture, needs, interests, and world if your manual doesn't do so. Show them that the content has personal meaning for them. Religion more than any other subject offers opportunities for this.

Add personal stories and examples to your lesson to make them more interesting. However, don't overdo it.

Weave information from the daily news into your lessons. Bring in an article from the local newspaper that is related to your topic and read it to the class.

Take advantage of special days and seasons and work them into your lessons. Use purple paper during Lent. Give out Thanksgiving stickers in November. Tell the story of St. Nicholas on his feast day.

Aim to have at least one activity in each lesson that children will consider fun and exciting. This will help them to look forward to your class.

Having a special visitor works wonders, too, especially if it is a parent. The novelty of a new person in the class charms some children away from misbehavior. It also motivates you to produce a better-than-usual lesson!

✔*Make them challenging.* Activities that are too difficult are frustrating, but those that are too simple are boring. Children are flattered by challenging demands. Challenges keep the brighter students from becoming smart alecks or reading a book under their desks.

Ask questions that involve critical thinking—questions that begin with *how* or *why.*

Plan activities that call for initiative and creativity.

Sometimes challenge children to compete against a clock. For example, say, "See if you can answer all ten questions in five minutes."

✔*Be sure they are complete.* Make each lesson a complete entity that does not depend on a previous lesson or the next lesson. Some children are often absent, especially those who are sometimes at the home of their other parent. With lessons that are complete in themselves, these children will not feel left out when they return.

Tips for planning good lessons

Try the following for planning the best possible lessons.

• Use the manual your program provides. It offers lessons that are well worked out and include many good ideas.

• Begin with something that will immediately intrigue children.

• Rehearse your lessons mentally in order to plan specific directions, foresee problems, and imagine your class's reactions.

• Plan your lessons to make sure that children experience success. Students who continually fail become dissatisfied. Their negative feelings lead to problems.

• Have a back-up plan or "ice-box plan" in case a prepared lesson cannot be carried out: if a speaker does not arrive or if you do not have time to prepare the week's lesson, for example.

• Write an outline of your plan on a card to guide you during the class.

Teach a smooth, lively lesson

Once I observed a primary class in which the teacher talked for forty minutes, asking questions every now and then. The children were literally falling out of their seats, while I was falling asleep.

At the outset give children a preview of what they will be doing during the lesson. Keep them apprised of the stages of the lesson so they can feel that progress is being made. Make remarks like "There is only one more section to read." Maintain a sure, brisk pace. Your tone of voice and the rate at which you speak can make the difference between bright-eyed children and sleepy ones.

Move smoothly and quickly from one activity to another with no gaps of time in which the children can entertain themselves. Have all your materials organized and ready to use. Avoid flip-flopping, or mixing lesson parts. For example, don't make comments such as, "When we were discussing page 3 fifteen minutes ago, I forgot to mention...."

In giving directions, wait until you have every child's attention. Then give clear, definite directions in as few words as possible. Otherwise you will face a barrage of questions and a room full of buzzing children trying to clarify for one another what to do. Give directions only once. You might have a child repeat them. Then ask if there are any questions. Whenever directions involve a page in the books, write the page number on the board and circle it for easy reference.

Don't distribute materials until it is time to use them or the children will play with them, read them, and be distracted while you want their undivided attention.

Ways to keep children alert

Try the following methods to keep those you teach on their toes at all times.

Come up with surprises. Award special prizes. Have an unusual object displayed that is related to the lesson, but don't explain it until it is time. Celebrate odd events such as reaching page 100 in the textbook. Introduce incongruity into the class unexpectedly to capture attention. For example, begin speaking pig-Latin, pretend to be a magician, or tell a short joke. Surprises help make classes fun and exciting.

Call on students at random. Ask the question first and

then call a name to keep all the students thinking. You might use a set of cards with their names, and call the names as you turn over the cards so that everyone must answer eventually. Sometimes draw a card from the back of the pile so that children who have already answered must remain alert. However you choose to call on them, try not to call the same ones all the time. This smacks of favoritism. To encourage the students to listen to one another, occasionally ask a student if he or she agrees with the answer just given.

Ask the whole class to respond. Address questions to the entire class for which they will respond by a show of hands. For example, ask "How many of you think that David is a real hero?"

Evaluate your lessons

In the course of each lesson you teach, monitor its success. When children are restless or bored, acknowledge the fact. You might even ask them why they feel that way. Then make a change in your plan to gain their attention—even a drastic change. For example, stop reading the textbook and have the children stand and add gestures to a religious song or hold an unexpected review with rapid-fire questions.

After class reflect on the lesson. Plan ways to improve discipline during the next lesson.

For Your Reflection

✔How much time do you spend preparing your lessons? Do you feel it is enough? Why or why not?

_____

_____

_____

_____

_____

✔If you were a child in your class how would you feel about your lessons? Be honest!

_____

_____

_____

_____

_____

✔What grade do you think the children in your class would give you for your lessons? How might they grade your attitude toward them?

_____

_____

_____

_____

_____

Leaning on Others

A legend relates what happened when Jesus first appeared in heaven after his death and resurrection. An angel met him and seeing his wounds, said, "You must have suffered terribly down there. Does everyone on Earth know how much you love them?" Jesus answered, "No, just a few in a corner of Palestine. But I've asked Peter, James, John, and the other apostles to tell others. Then these will tell others until everyone has heard the story."

But the angel knew human beings and asked, "What if the apostles forget? What if the others fail to tell about you and your sacrifice? Have you made any other plans?"

"I have no other plans," replied Jesus. "I'm counting on them."

Christianity is a religion of interdependence. Jesus counts on us to carry on his work of teaching. We in turn can count on others to help us fulfill this all-important, awesome ministry.

DREs, principals, and religion teachers are supportive people. So, when you feel that your class is getting out of control, or you are at your wits' end because of a certain child's behavior, don't let pride keep you from getting help. Asking for help is not a sign of weakness, but indicates a desire to improve. You will be doing yourself and your students a favor. Don't wait until your class is utter chaos and unbearable. Before seeking outside help, however, make sure you have tried private talks with thoses who are causing you problems.

Contact parents

Your best recourse is to contact parents. Parents know their children better than we do. They are the primary educators of their children. Set up a conference. One phone call might make the difference. When one boy's behavior became intolerable, I called his mother and asked if she had any suggestions. She merely said, "Don't worry. I'll take care of this." Before the next class, the boy apologized to me and became a model student. When there were lapses in his behavior, I simply had to say, "Do I have to call home again?" and he would toe the line.

Approach parents with the attitude that together you can work to solve the problem. You may find out that they are aware of the problem already and can give you advice. They may inform you of other factors that will shed light on the problem and help you to understand the child better. If parents are skeptical or difficult to talk to, that might be a clue to the child's behavior.

In talking to parents be honest. Don't skirt the issue. Be able to back up what you say with specific examples. Try to be tactful. Use positive expressions about their children. At the end of a phone conversation with parents, let them hang up first.

Following are a few harsh and gentle ways to phrase the bald truth:

Negative	More positive
lazy	can do more if he or she tries
cheats	wasn't honest
rude	inconsiderate
trouble maker	disturbs the class
lies	stretches the truth
mean	has difficulty in getting along
selfish	seldom shares
shows off	tries to get attention
wastes time	could make better use of time
never does the right thing	can learn to do the right thing
often interrupts	enjoys offering his or her opinions

Hold a conference with the child and parents, thus providing an opportunity to talk about the problem. Invite the child to clarify his or her feelings and together face the situation constructively.

When parents have been involved in helping you solve a problem, contact them with feedback on how their child is improving. This shows them you care about their child and not just his or her behavior.

Appeal to administrators

Your DRE, religion coordinator, and principal are all

there for you. They will be glad to help. Consult them about your discipline problems. Invite them into your class to observe or to teach a lesson for you. You might tape a lesson (audio or video) and go through it with them. The source of your problem may be an annoying mannerism you are not even aware of that could easily be eliminated from your teaching.

Send misbehaving children to administrators for help in solving the problem, not for punishment. Try to take care of your own punishments. Be aware that sending children to the DRE or principal might weaken their regard for you.

Use peer support

Your colleagues will sympathize with you and support you. Ask them for advice. Be willing to share with them what has worked for you. Talk out frustrations with a co-worker, one who can give sound advice as well as bolster your morale. He or she might share horror stories that top your own!

Visit the classes of other teachers or catechists. Through observing good teachers, you will glean tricks of the trade for maintaining discipline. You will also develop a sense for the friendly, but businesslike style of teaching that creates a healthy atmosphere.

A priest or a counselor might also be able to help you cope with discipline problems and offer advice. Your own family members, who probably know you through and through, can possibly give you insight into your classroom problems.

Sometimes you will be able to enlist the help of other children to guide a student to better behavior. An appeal to the whole class for their opinion of a misdeed is effective in stopping it when you don't know the guilty person.

Attend lectures and read books and magazines that provide information on being a good teacher and suggestions for discipline. A marvelous book is *You Can Handle Them All* written by Robert L. DeBruyn and Jack L. Larson. This handbook describes more than one hundred problem behaviors and recommends specific techniques to manage each one. It is published by The Master Teacher, Inc.; Leadership Lane, P.O. Box 1207; Manhattan, KS 66502.

Call on the Holy Spirit

Finally, rely on the Holy Spirit for help. You might wish to adopt or write a special prayer to tap into supernatural power before teaching each class. Here is a sample:

Holy Spirit, be with me as I share in the work of Jesus. Let the truths I teach sink into the minds and hearts of my students. May they come to know your love and to follow your way. Amen.

Trust God to draw good out of your disasters. A colleague counseled me one day: "Remember that you are an instrument of God. The Holy Spirit is acting in you to touch their lives in ways that you may never know. Trust God, do your best, and don't worry."

Pray for your students as well as for yourself. One wise catechist advised, "Spend more time talking to God about your students than you spend talking to your students about God."

Keep children's names in your prayer book or in your plan book. Before preparing a lesson, pray for each child individually—each of them, the model students and the monsters. Praying for your students may change your attitude toward them if nothing else, and that could make all the difference in the world.

For Your Reflection

✔What can you do to remind yourself that you do not teach alone but with God's help? Which of the suggestions in this chapter would work best for you?

_____

_____

_____

_____

_____

✔To whom can you go for help with discipline in your situation? Have you tried talking to your DRE or principal? Have you talked to veteran teachers to get their advice? If not, make a resolution to do so as soon as possible.

_____

_____

_____

_____

_____

✔Do you ever go directly to parents when you have a problem? Why or why not? What has been the result?

_____

_____

_____

_____

_____

8

Involving the Children

Most children are less likely to cause trouble if they have a sense of belonging or ownership and if they are kept busy. Involving children in activities fills both of these needs. In addition, activities promote learning. Students supposedly remember twenty percent of what they hear but eighty percent of what they do.

Invite participation in class planning
Give children a say in setting the standards for the class or for certain activities. Before a group discussion, for instance, ask them to propose guidelines to follow and have a secretary list these at the board.

Offer a choice of activities: "Do you want to

watch a video or put on a play?" "Would you rather write a report or give an oral report?" Also give children choices in minor matters. Ask, "Do you wish to work alone or in groups, in pencil or pen, on colored paper or white?"

Keep children active

Channel their natural tendencies and characteristic energy to accomplish your lesson's goals. Hold activities that allow talking: discussions, group projects, artwork. Invite questions and comments during the lesson. Be careful though that children don't always sidetrack you so that the lesson's objectives are not achieved.

Never tell children anything they can tell you. Instead of giving a summary of a paragraph, ask them for one. Instead of reviewing what was studied in the last lesson, let them do it. After you pose a question, allow sufficient "think time" and be comfortable with the silence instead of answering the question yourself.

Incorporate activities that engage children in other kinds of physical activity: singing, walking to the board, putting on plays, role-playing, racing, making something.

Never do something that children can do for themselves, even if you think you can do it faster or better. Let them pass out papers, write on the board, draw a transparency, read from the Bible, or run the projectors. Having children operate the equipment also frees you to supervise the class better.

If they are reading their text, direct them to highlight key words, underline sentences, number facts, and put notes in the margins as they go along. Occasionally let individual children be the teacher for a while. You will see yourself reflected in their voices and style of teaching.

Try cooperative learning

Cooperative learning worked for me when I taught a class of "low-track" freshmen. At a teacher-parent conference I discovered that a ninth grader named Martha was a headache for all of her teachers except me.

That year I was experimenting with group work. Each week my students chose activities from a list and worked together to carry them out. In this setting, Martha blossomed. One day I even overheard her scolding the others in her group, "Be quiet. I want to do this."

Plan for cooperative learning. Let students work with partners or in groups. At times make each group responsible for teaching something to the whole class. Find a project for the students to work on together, perhaps a parish activity. An added advantage of cooperative learning is that it teaches skills and virtues that are basic for Christian community.

By the way, when two children have a disagreement or a fight and disrupt the class, have them talk to one another until they can settle their disagreement. Encourage them and advise them as they work to find a solution to their problem, but don't do it for them.

Employ conflict resolution methods

Principals and teachers are finding conflict resolution and mediation methods very effective in diffusing situations that involve two or more angry students. Teachers trained in these methods function as peacemakers rather than law enforcers. In addition, children learn to handle their problems in a mature and Christian way.

At one school I know of, the junior-high students were upset because one girl threatened to beat up another girl at a school dance. The principal brought the two girls together and worked through the process of mediation with happy results. Of their own accord, after leaving the office the two girls visited each junior-high class and apologized for the trouble they had caused. Moreover, after the dance the aggressor made it a point to tell the principal how much she had enjoyed the dance.

The following steps of conflict resolution are adapted from a pioneed school program that has proved very successful. (See *Conflict Resolution: An Elementary School Curriculum* reprinted with permission by The Community Board Program, 1540 Market Street, 490, San Francisco, CA 94102, chapter 6, ©1990).

1. Both students agree on these three ground rules: Each one states, "I agree not to interrupt, not to name call, and I agree to work to resolve the conflict.

2. One person tells his or her side of the story using "I-messages," statements that begin with "I," not "You." The person includes how he or she feels and what he or she wants.

3. The second person restates what the first person said. He or she may begin with "So the problem for you is...." and may ask questions to understand the situation better.

4. The second persons tells his or her side of the story using "I-messages."

5. The first person restates what the second person said and may ask questions.

6. Both persons suggest solutions that will help both.

7. Both persons work to agree on a resolution. The resolution should
   • be specific, with all the details spelled out.
   • be balanced, so that both people share the responsibility for making it work.
   • be realistic
   • solve the problem and address underlying issue

In preparation for the meeting, you can have the children fill out forms on which they complete statements like "I have a problem with... and "Two solutions for my problem are...."

In mediating between two young children, the steps can be shortened to these three:

1. Each student says how he or she feels, what happened, and what he or she wants.

2. Each student suggests something he or she can do to solve the problem.

3. Both students work together to agree on a resolution.

Often it is sufficient to have the young victim tell how he or she felt when an incident happened and then ask the other child how he or she feels now. Most likely the little attacker will immediately express regret.

You might want to investigate local teacher-training courses in conflict resolution and mediation. You can find out more about these methods by contacting the organizations listed on pages 97 under "Organizations for Conflict Resolution."

Include everyone

Make it a point to call on every child during class. Match the level of questions to the ability of the students so that poorer students can answer correctly and experience success.

When you speak to the class look at all the students, not down at the floor, at a spot above their heads, or at a select few students. Avoid favoritism. It will turn the class against you.

After an activity, ask the students to comment on their behavior and how it could be improved. Periodically assess together how the goals set at the beginning of the year are being met.

For Your Reflection

✔ Are there things you've been doing in class that students would be able to do for themselves? Why do you think you do this?

_____

_____

_____

_____

_____

✔ What topics in your curriculum lend themselves to cooperative learning? Have you already experimented with this type of learning? With what result?

_____

_____

_____

_____

_____

✔ Do you try to keep children as active as possible as they go through your lessons? What techniques work for you?

_____

_____

_____

_____

_____

9

Noticing Absolutely Everything

The comment about teachers having eyes in back of their heads is not farfetched. A good teacher tries to see and hear everything that's going on. Make sure though that you see what you think you see and interpret it correctly. Avoid jumping to conclusions. Once while teaching class, out of the corner of my eye I saw two people disappear through the forbidden door in the hall that led to the roof. Having caught two students the day before dropping erasers off the roof, I ran to the door and called out, "Just where do you think you're going?" Two men appeared and introduced themselves as diocesan officials surveying the building.

Always try to be observant

We can be so engrossed in our lessons that we fail to notice other things like Larry's setting fire to Jim's pants with a lighter. Being well prepared frees us to give more attention to those we teach. When our eyes aren't glued to our manual or plan, we can glance around the class and make eye contact where necessary.

Stand while teaching in order to have a better view of the class. Periodically scan the class as you teach. Circulate among children during the lesson. This will keep you in touch with what's happening and will squelch many an unwelcome activity. It will also force children to turn their heads and move their eyes. If you always teach behind a desk, both you and the children will quickly become bored.

Here are other ways you can be observant:

• If you can't turn your back on your class to write on the board, use an overhead projector instead.

• Always look ahead. If an upcoming lesson, prayer service, or movie includes a section that will induce puzzlement, consternation, or a strong reaction in your students, prepare them for it.

• Try to deal with more than one issue at a time. Observing how adroit you are at doing two acts simultaneously, children are less apt to disrupt the learning process with misbehavior. They'll know you can handle them.

• Stop undesirable activity immediately, nonverbally if possible. If it continues, other children will soon imitate the activity, and your problems will quickly multiply.

• When children are doing independent work or group work, keep an eye on them. Better still, be with them. Just because they're busy, don't use this time to prepare your next lesson or to read a novel at your desk.

Overlook things (sometimes)

Sometimes there are good reasons to ignore misbehavior during class. Maybe the "crime" is not serious, and stopping to take note of it will cause more disruption than ignoring it. Also, your calling attention to it might be just what the child wants. Creating a scene would give him or her attention, but it might also destroy the learning process.

You may need more time to evaluate the situation. Besides, a problem that seems like a disaster at the end of a hard day can shrink to molehill size after a rest. Weigh all the factors and use good judgment in determining whether it is worthwhile to correct a child during class should the same behavior come up again.

Apply whenever possible the motto of Pope John XXIII: "See everything. Overlook much. Correct a little."

Make notes regularly

It's important to take notes about what you observe as you teach. Try to develop a habit of doing this right after each class. Sometimes what you observe may give you insights about something you are doing wrong. If you notice that your children often seemed bored or unresponsive, you may need to vary your activities.

If you notice that a particular child has changed his or her behavior from friendly to withdrawn, you may want to contact his or her parents. If you're not observant, you won't even notice the change.

If you notice that a child is often the cause of disruptions during your lessons, you will want to note this and the circumstances so that you are prepared to explain or describe this behavior to parents as well as help the child. Be objective and record specific and significant acts. Write the dates and incidents of a child's offenses on a 3" x 5" file card.

Evaluate each lesson

Evaluate each lesson to become more aware of what went right and what went wrong and why. Consider how you handled individual cases of misbehavior. Determine ways you can improve.

For Your Reflection

✔How can you become better aware of what is going on in your class? What do you do now to keep aware?

_____
_____
_____
_____
_____

✔Are you willing to sometimes overlook minor problems? Why or why not?

_____
_____
_____
_____
_____

✔Do you regularly make notes about what goes on in your religion class? Would this be a valuable practice for you in the future?

_____
_____
_____
_____
_____

10

Emphasizing What's Good

The adage "You can catch more flies with a drop of honey than with a barrel of vinegar" holds true in the classroom. I remember once when I was a ninth grader, I had just finished sweeping the floor and my teacher said, "This floor is so clean you could eat off it." That comment made me feel proud—and determined to be the best floor sweeper ever for the rest of the year to keep up my reputation.

Reinforce good behavior

Positive words have positive reactions. Children love to be praised. So do adults for that matter. The man responsible for the art and design of some textbooks I was writing appreciated my positive comments on the page proofs. He cut them out and pinned them to the bulletin board in his office! Be lavish with praise but not dishonest. Children know when praise is deserved and when it is insincere praise used as a ploy.

Praise indicates success, the best motivator, and stimulates students to continue trying. Also, complimenting one child or a small group prods the rest of the class to imitate the behavior that is praised. Make a comment like "How hard the boys and girls in the third row are working!" and watch how the children in rows one, two, four, and five immediately settle down.

Give attention and praise to those who are doing the right thing and ignore those who are not. Unrewarded behaviors become extinct.

Occasionally comment on the entire class's good behavior. For example, say "I like the way everyone is working hard today." Be sure to praise the class when they have not been influenced by the misbehavior of one or a few students.

Here are some ways to offer praise:

- Give verbal praise during, before, or after class.
- Make it a habit to write positive comments on children's work. A "nice job" or "good thinking" at the top of a paper is worth the extra time it takes to write.
- Phone students at home to praise them for good behavior you noticed in your class. Or call their parents about something positive the students have done. They will be pleasantly surprised.
- Write a little note on special paper or a card to congratulate a child for good behavior or for a noticeable improvement.
- Display the students' work in the room and in the parish hall.

• Ask to keep some papers or artwork. The children will be pleased and proud.

In addition to praise, use other incentives for good behavior. Give out stars, stickers, and other small awards. Bestow privileges or let the children do something they like to do.

Row races are popular with younger children. Assign each row a number and write the number on the board. Periodically award a star to a row for such things as sitting tall, being ready to listen, trying to answer, or being quiet. At the end of the class or the week, give the winning row small prizes.

Make a badge out of cardboard with the initials RTG for Real Third Grader (or initials for the grade you teach). Cover the badge with clear contact paper and tape a safety pin on the back. At the end of each class give the badge to a student to take home for the week. Specify what the student did to deserve the badge.

Educational psychologists estimate that the ratio of negative teacher comments to positive teacher comments is 8 to 1. Tape a lesson. As you replay it, keep score on paper how many of your statements during a lesson were positive and how many were negative. Note missed opportunities to give your students a boost.

Be positive about yourself
Know that your ministry is challenging. Dick Van Dyke once described a teacher in words to this effect:

A teacher must have the faith of Abraham,
the patience of Job,
the wisdom of Solomon,
the courage of Daniel as he goes into the lions' den,
and the confidence of Moses that it is all worthwhile.

Evaluate yourself as a disciplinarian and notice small triumphs. Give yourself little rewards for accomplishments.

Make a Booster Box for yourself as a morale builder. Save tokens of your successes like thank-you notes from the students and words of praise from your colleagues. In hard times go through your collection and recall that you are good and do a fine job.

Keep things in perspective. Know that your students are not miniature adults. Also realize that not everyone in your class is delinquent. Focus on those children who are receptive and teach to them so that your efforts won't seem in vain, and you will be motivated to go on.

If you have an "impossible" class, and even if the DRE or principal is afraid to come into your room and if other catechists refer to your class as "wild animals," persevere. Muster reserve supplies of enthusiasm and hide your feelings of defeat. A sense of humor may save you, whereas breaking down before the children in rage or in tears of frustration puts the reins of control firmly in their hands.

Learn to take criticism

Take criticism from students and parents with a grain of salt. Look for objective proof. Once during a phone call with an Italian mother whose daughter was a classroom menace, I was told: "Ann and her friends say you favor the Black students." That very night I was at a parent conference for a Black girl in the same class and her mother charged, "You are known to pick on the Black students."

If you come prepared to do your best and don't take the class's failures as personal failures, you will manage to be at peace. Remember, your students' behavior is not against you personally, but against your authority role.

Seldom is the behavior meant to hurt you. Someday you may laugh at these experiences. In the meantime make yourself a sign that says "This too will pass."

Whatever you do, don't quit. You have a lot to offer, and the church needs you.

Enjoy your job

Being a catechist can be an enjoyable and fulfilling ministry. If you are finding it a chore or a burden and can hardly wait until class is over each week, figure out why. It may be that you are doing too much and do not have the time to be a successful teacher. Or perhaps you would be better working with a different grade level. Maybe a change in content would be good.

Take whatever measures you can to be a joyful, dedicated Christian, eager to share the Good News of Jesus Christ. It's well worth it. At those times when you are tempted to get discouraged, remember these words of Paul to Timothy (paraphrased):

"Your role is so important. I implore you to continue to proclaim God's Word; be persistent in your teaching, whether it is convenient or inconvenient. Do everything you can to convince, reprimand, and encourage children to hear the truth. Above all, be very patient with them" (2 Timothy 4:2).

For Your Reflection

✔ Would you consider yourself a negative or positive teacher? Why do you think this is so?

_____

_____

_____

_____

_____

✔ Do you tend to focus on the difficult aspects of your ministry or the positive ones? Have you ever tried the "Booster Box" suggestion?

_____

_____

_____

_____

_____

✔ How do you react to Paul's words to Timothy? Do you pray often for a joyful heart? Why not start today?

_____

_____

_____

_____

_____

Conclusion

As I am writing this, the Winter Olympics are taking place in Lillehammer, Norway. The world is witnessing the fruit of many years of discipline on the part of those champions competing for medals. St. Paul reminds us, "Every athlete exercises discipline in every way. They do it to win a perishable crown but we an imperishable one" (1 Corinthians 9:25). As catechists we practice discipline, trying to instill discipline in those we teach.

After all, we are going for the gold. We are determined to be good religion teachers who form new generations of faithful, dedicated Christians on fire with love for God and others. We are willing to give our all in carrying out Christ's command to teach others about the great love God has for us.

We are convinced of the importance of imparting to our children the values, morals, and virtues needed to live happily and to heal this world's wounds. These crucial goals as well as our ultimate goal, our own salvation, motivate and energize us. And the means of these goals is discipline, our own and our students'.

Not an easy task

Of course, our task is difficult and demanding—even more so than landing a triple Axel on ice. Jesus never said that sharing his message would be easy. Instead he talked about being insulted and persecuted, taking up the cross, shaking dust off our feet from towns that rejected his teaching, and being sent like sheep in the midst of wolves! At times we feel overwhelmed and discouraged.

Thinking we are not accomplishing anything, we are tempted to quit. Especially at these times it is good to remember that we are only called to do our best—and then leave the rest up to God. In the end we all must echo Paul's words: "I planted the seed and Apollos watered it, but God made it grow" (1 Corinthians 3:6). It is God who is the real coach.

If you are a beginning catechist, you might be wondering how you will ever be able to put into practice everything in this book. I recommend concentrating on one or two chapters a year, beginning with chapter 3, "Starting Off Right." With time, experience, and a little help from friends, you will probably develop into a master catechist.

Beatitudes for religion teachers

In the meantime, as you practice the fine art of discipline, you might ponder the following Beatitudes for religion teachers. They recap some of the main concepts in this book:

Happy are the organized and prepared, for their lessons will run smoothly, leaving no time for the children to get into mischief or even to think about it.

Happy are the creative, careful lesson planners, for they will hold their children's attention and their classes will not be boring.

Happy are the observing and alert, for they will be aware of their class's moods and activities and prevent many problems.

Happy are the loving, caring teachers, for their students will try not to disappoint them.

Happy are the firm and fair, for they will listen and be listened to.

Happy are those who discipline with respect for the child, for respect will be given them.

Happy are those who teach with enthusiasm, for their children will catch their spirit and grow in faith.

Happy are teachers who continue to learn, for so will their students—with peace, joy, and satisfaction.

May this book help you to carry out your significant role as a catechist in the church and may it also help you to fulfill these words:

"You will shine in the world like bright stars because you are offering it the word of life" (Philippians 2:15–16).

Resources

Helpful articles on the practical aspects of teaching are often found in *Religion Teacher's Journal* and *Catechist*. In addition, you may want to consult some of the following books for more information.

Albert, Linda. *A Teacher's Guide to Cooperative Discipline*. Circle Pines, Minnesota: American Guidance Service, 1989.

Alfonso, Regina Marie, S.N.D. *How Jesus Taught*. Staten Island, N.Y.: Alba House, 1986.

Carducci, Dewey J. *The Caring Classroom*. Palo Alto, Calif.: Bull Publishing Company, 1984.

Community Board Program. *Conflict Resolution Elementary School Curriculum*. San Francisco, 1990.

Curwin, Richard L. and Mendler, A.N. *The*

Discipline Book: A Complete Guide to School and Classroom Management. Reston, Virginia: Reston Publishing Company, 1980.

DeBruyn, Robert L. and Jack L. Larson. *You Can Handle Them All.* Manhattan, Kansas: Master Teacher, 1984.

Dreikurs, Rudolf and L. Grey. *A New Approach to Discipline: Logical Consequences.* New York: Hawthorn Books, 1968.

Dues, Greg. *Teaching Religion with Confidence and Joy.* Mystic, Conn.: Twenty-Third Publications, 1988.

Ginott, Haim G. *Teacher and Child: A Book for Parents and Teachers.* New York: Macmillan Company, 1972.

Goldstein, Sam and Michael Goldstein. *Managing Attention Disorders in Children: A Guide for Practitioners.* New York: Wiley-Interscience Press.

Kounin, Jacob S. *Discipline and Group Management in Classrooms.* New York: Holt, Rinehart, and Winston. 1970.

McCarty, Jim. *The Confident Catechist.* Dubuque: Brown-ROA, 1990.

Manternach, Janaan and Carl Pfeifer. *Creative Catechist: A Comprehensive, Illustrated Guide for Religion Teachers.* Mystic, Conn.: Twenty-Third Publications, 1991.

O'Neal, Debbie. *More Than Glue and Glitter: A Classroom Guide for Volunteer Teachers.* Minneapolis: Augsburg Books, 1992.

Savage, Tom V. *Discipline for Self-Control.* Englewood Cliffs, N.J.: Prentice Hall, 1991.

Schippe, Cullen. *Planting, Watering, Growing! The Volunteer Catechist's Companion.* Granada Hills, CA: Sandalprints Publishing, 1990.

Schmidt, Fran and Alice Friedman. Abrams Peace Education Foundation. *Creative Conflict Solving for Kids, grades 4-9*. Grace Contrino, 1985.

Salvin, Robert, and others. *Learning to Cooperate, Cooperating to Learn*. New York: Plenum Press, 1985.

van Bemmel, John G. *Take Heart, Catechist: Twenty Stories for Guidance and Growth*. Mystic, Conn.: Twenty-Third Publications, 1991.

Walters, Thomas P. and Rita Tyson Walters. *Working Smarter, Not Harder*. Huntington, Ind.: Our Sunday Visitor, 1991.

Organizations for Conflict Resolution
Children's Creative Response to Conflict Program. Fellowship of Reconciliation, Box 271, Nyack, N.Y. 10960; (914) 358-4601.

The Community Board Program, 1540 Market Street, 490, San Francisco, CA 94102, (415) 552-1250.

Educators for Social Responsibility, School Conflict Resolution Programs, 23 Garden St., Cambridge, MA 02138; (617) 492-1764.

National Association for Mediation in Education (NAME), 205 Hampshire House, Box 33635, Amherst, MA 01003-3635; (413) 545-2462.

Also by Sr. Mary Kathleen Glavich...

Leading Students Into Prayer
Ideas and Suggestions from A to Z
Glavich explores the varied forms that prayer takes—personal and communal, vocal and mental, liturgical, Scripture-based, centering and traditional—and how to teach these techniques to children.
ISBN: 0-89622-549-6, 160 pp, $12.95

Leading Students Into Scripture
This book presents a wide range of methods to help children understand and appreciate the Bible.
ISBN: 0-89622-328-0, 112 pp, $9.95

Gospel Plays for Students
36 Scripts for Education & Worship
Here is a combination of popularly-known and less well-recognized gospel events that are scripted in easy-to-understand language.
ISBN: 0-89622-407-4, 112 pp, $12.95

Acting Out the Miracles and Parables
This book contains 52 playlets for grades 1-12 that will enliven and enrich religion classes.
ISBN: 0-89622-363-9, 142 pp, $12.95

Available at religious bookstores or from
TWENTY-THIRD PUBLICATIONS
P.O. Box 180 • Mystic, CT 06355
1-800-321-0411